DATE DUE	
SEP 1 7 2011		
DEC 1 7 2011	NOV 2 9 2011	

The Urbana Free Library

To renew materials call
217-367-4057

Adrenaline Adventure

Running the Rapids:
White-water Rafting, Canoeing, and Kayaking

Jeff C. Young
ABDO Publishing Company

visit us at
www.abdopublishing.com

Published by ABDO Publishing Company, 8000 West 78th Street, Edina, Minnesota 55439.

Printed in the United States of America, North Mankato, Minnesota.
092010
012011

 PRINTED ON RECYCLED PAPER

Cover Photo: iStockphoto
Interior Photos: Alamy pp. 12, 15; Corbis pp. 10–11; Getty Images pp. 25, 26, 27;
    iStockphoto pp. 1, 4–5, 8–9, 17; National Geographic Stock pp. 7, 20–21;
    Photolibrary pp. 14, 19, 29, 31; Thinkstock p. 22

Series Coordinator: Heidi M.D. Elston
Editors: Megan M. Gunderson, BreAnn Rumsch
Art Direction & Cover Design: Neil Klinepier

Library of Congress Cataloging-in-Publication Data

Young, Jeff C., 1948-
  Running the rapids : white-water rafting, canoeing, and kayaking / Jeff C. Young.
    p. cm. -- (Adrenaline adventure)
  Includes bibliographical references and index.
  ISBN 978-1-61613-551-5 (alk. paper)
  1. White-water canoeing--Juvenile literature. I. Title.
  GV788.Y68 2011
  797.1'22--dc22
                          2010028240

Contents

Early Running

Thousands of years ago, people began making the earliest canoes and kayaks. They hollowed out large tree trunks and floated them down waterways. Early humans used these vessels for hunting, fishing, and transportation. The boats were heavy and difficult to carry. But they got the job done.

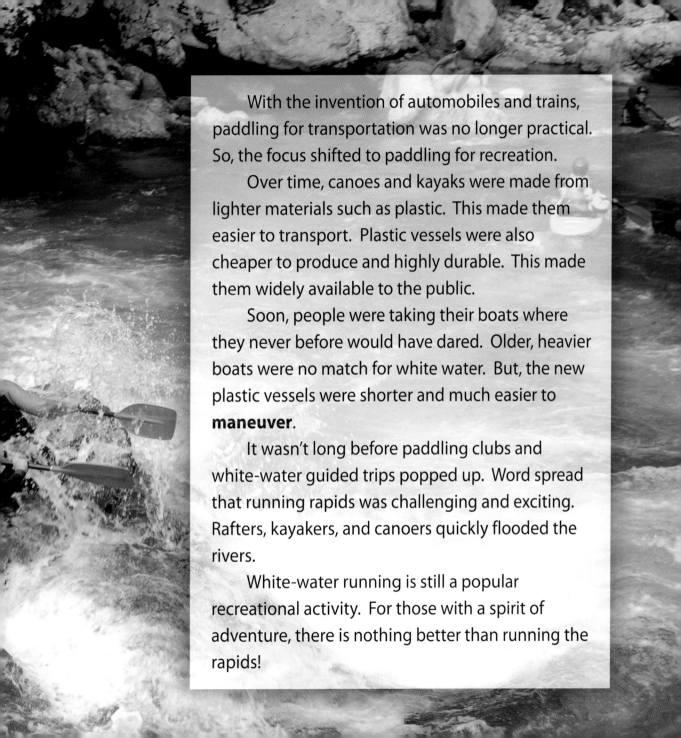

With the invention of automobiles and trains, paddling for transportation was no longer practical. So, the focus shifted to paddling for recreation.

Over time, canoes and kayaks were made from lighter materials such as plastic. This made them easier to transport. Plastic vessels were also cheaper to produce and highly durable. This made them widely available to the public.

Soon, people were taking their boats where they never before would have dared. Older, heavier boats were no match for white water. But, the new plastic vessels were shorter and much easier to **maneuver**.

It wasn't long before paddling clubs and white-water guided trips popped up. Word spread that running rapids was challenging and exciting. Rafters, kayakers, and canoers quickly flooded the rivers.

White-water running is still a popular recreational activity. For those with a spirit of adventure, there is nothing better than running the rapids!

River Grading

White-water running involves paddling canoes, kayaks, or rafts down fast-moving, turbulent rivers. Not all rivers are created equal. Rivers are rated at six levels of difficulty. Before starting any run, find out the river's rating. Do not run a river that is above your skill level. This could mean the difference between life and death.

From easiest to hardest, rivers range from Class I to Class VI. A Class I river is called easy. It will have small waves and few, if any, obstacles. This is where a beginner should learn to run. Class II is a river with some obstacles and waves less than two feet (0.6 m) high. Class II has a rating of novice.

Class III is for rivers of medium difficulty with waves up to three feet (0.9 m) high. The rapids have recognizable passages and require **maneuvering** around obstacles. These intermediate courses are for experienced paddlers.

Class IV is advanced, and Class V is rated expert. Both have many obstacles and strong waves. Class V rivers will also have big drops and very strong currents.

Class VI simply means the river is too dangerous for rafting, kayaking, or canoeing. These rivers are rated daredevil! Even expert runners are warned to avoid Class VI white water.

Paddlers need to know how to read a river. This involves determining the direction of the current and looking for any dangers. Experienced paddlers plan a safe route and remain in control.

Playing It Safe

Even on a Class I river, the biggest danger white-water runners face is drowning. That is why life jackets are a must! Also, paddlers should never go boating alone. All paddlers should be good swimmers. Unexpected swims are always possible!

Most injuries on the water occur because of exhaustion. Being in good shape is a big part of being a successful paddler. That doesn't mean you have to be a body builder! But you do need strength, **flexibility**, and **endurance**. This will help you avoid injury.

All white-water running involves common **hazards** you must avoid. These include siphons, strainers, and sweepers. Unfortunately, people use rivers for dumping junk cars, appliances, and other objects. Watch out for debris sticking out of the water and steer clear! Getting in the habit of constantly looking downstream will help you stay safe.

Most of the time, staying safe is just a matter of common sense. Understand your abilities. Avoid pushing yourself beyond your limits. Don't be foolish, and don't take needless risks.

LINGO

EDDY - often a safe place for a boat to get out of the current. It is a place where water flows back upstream, such as behind a rock or other obstacle.

PORTAGE - to carry boats on land around a difficult part of a river.

PUT-IN - the river access where a trip begins.

RUN - a section of a river that can be boated.

SIPHON - where water disappears underground. Paddlers can quickly be sucked down, too.

STRAINER - any obstacle that allows water to pass through but not boats or people.

SWEEPER - trees that have fallen into a river but are still rooted to the bank.

SWIMMER - a person who has fallen out of the boat.

TAKE-OUT - the river access where a trip ends.

WRAP - a boat held against a rock or other obstacle by the force of the current.

The Boat

The boat is a runner's main piece of equipment. Canoes, kayaks, and rafts are all popular white-water boats.

White-water runners wishing to run rapids in a canoe can choose from decked or open canoes. Decked canoes have decks that keep out water. They look a lot like kayaks. Open canoes are open on top. They have no deck, so they can easily fill with water. White-water paddlers stuff air bags into any open spaces to avoid this.

White-water canoes are often made of lightweight materials such as plastic or fiberglass. The body of the canoe is called the hull. The front end is called the bow, and the back is the stern. From bow to stern, white-water canoes vary in length.

The ends of white-water canoes are usually raised out of the water. The degree to which the ends are raised is called rocker. Canoes that have a lot of rocker can spin and turn more easily. This lessens the chance of hitting any obstacles!

Air bags are secured to the canoe to keep out water and help the boat stay light.

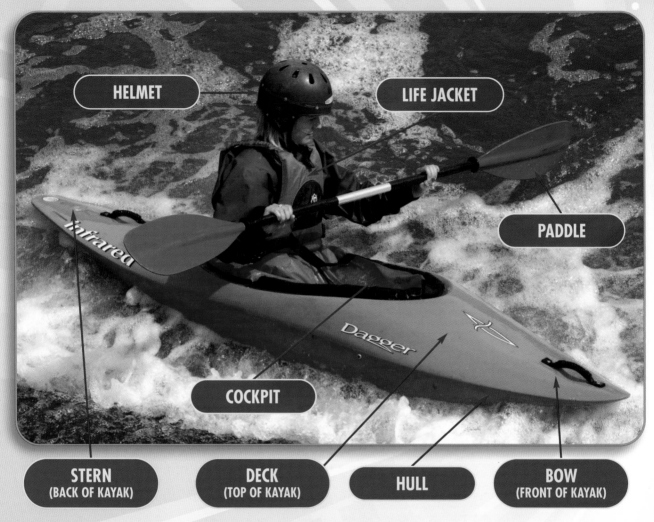

HELMET

LIFE JACKET

PADDLE

COCKPIT

STERN
(BACK OF KAYAK)

DECK
(TOP OF KAYAK)

HULL

BOW
(FRONT OF KAYAK)

Some people like white-water kayaks. These boats are made of plastic and are highly **maneuverable**. White-water kayaks are about 8.5 feet (2.5 m) long. Kayaks are built to be buoyant. That means they will still float even if they are swamped with water.

The top of the kayak is called the deck. Within the deck there is a hollowed-out area for the kayaker to sit. It's called the cockpit. Most kayaks have one cockpit, but some models have two or four.

Inside, kayaks have strong footrests and back straps. This gives paddlers something to brace against as they fight rapids. There should also be plenty of padding inside. It holds the paddler in place.

Many people choose to run a river with a group of friends in a raft. Rafts used for white-water runs are **inflatable**. They range in length from 10 to 20 feet (3 to 6 m) or more. White-water rafts need to be very sturdy. They must also keep air in and water out. So, they have a rubberized coating.

Paddle rafts and oar rafts are the two basic types of rafts used for white-water trips. Most commercial guide services use paddle rafts. They usually seat four to eight people plus a river guide.

On a paddle raft, the passengers are part of the crew! They use paddles to guide and **propel** the raft. As a team, they listen for the guide's instructions for navigating the rushing water.

An oar raft seats three to five people. On this type of boat, the guide does all the work. The guide controls two long oars while the passengers sit back and enjoy the ride!

The Gear

Spray skirts work to keep paddlers dry even in the roughest waters.

On fast-moving rivers, you need special gear to keep you safe and dry. A personal flotation device (PFD) is the most important piece of equipment a runner can have. It will keep you afloat if your boat **capsizes**. Always wear a PFD, even if you are a strong swimmer. Even the best swimmer can get swept away in a swiftly moving current.

A helmet is another essential piece of equipment. It should fit snugly enough that it won't move when you shake your head. A wet suit will protect your body from cold water. Gloves will protect your hands.

To move your boat through the water, you need a paddle. White-water canoers and rafters use a single-blade paddle to **propel** and steer. A kayaker uses a paddle with a blade at each end.

In kayaks and decked canoes, white-water paddlers use spray skirts to stay dry. A spray skirt fits around your waist and attaches to the cockpit rim. It keeps waves from lapping into your boat. The spray skirt should fit you snugly. It should not come off the cockpit rim unless you pull hard.

If you're on a raft with several other people, a spray skirt just won't work. That's when a bailing bucket comes in handy. Use it to remove water that has lapped over the raft's sides. One gallon (4 L) of water weighs about eight pounds (4 kg). The added weight slows down the raft and makes it harder to steer.

A life jacket and the right paddle are important. Don't forget to strap on your helmet!

Let's Race!

For some, the thrill of running the rapids for the fun of it is not enough. Luckily, there are different types of competitions available to these paddlers. Popular events include slalom, sprint, and downriver races. They test a racer's strength, **endurance**, and skills.

Slalom is a style of racing in which runners **maneuver** through pairs of poles called gates. Paddlers zigzag through the gates as fast as they can without touching or missing any. Competitors who touch or completely miss a gate receive time penalties.

Sprint events involve racing against other teams. Racers must paddle hard and fast to come out on top. Downriver racing is the most demanding. These events take paddlers through some of the roughest waters.

In all types of racing, runners should practice good sportsmanship. Racers cannot intentionally interfere with other competitors or leave their assigned racing lanes. Individuals or teams that do not respect the rules earn time penalties. They can even be **disqualified** from events.

Slalom racers must conquer rapids, waves, eddies, and strong currents as they paddle through gates.

Paddle Power

Whether paddling for fun or to win, it is important to warm up. Jogging and jumping jacks get your blood pumping before you hit the water. After that, stretch your muscles from head to toe. Once you are warmed up, safely seat yourself in your boat. You're ready to start paddling!

In a canoe or a raft, you will use a single-blade paddle. Place one hand on the grip, or the top of the paddle. Your knuckles should be facing upward with the thumb under. Place the other hand midway down the paddle's shaft just above the blade. When your right hand is on the grip, paddle on the boat's left side. If your left hand is on the grip, paddle on the right side.

The forward stroke is the most common stroke in canoeing and kayaking. It moves the boat forward. To do this when canoeing, lean forward from your hips. Extend your lower arm forward and place the blade in the water. The farther forward you reach, the more power you will get.

Your guide may have you practice your paddling on dry land before heading down the river.

Once the blade is in the water, pull back with your lower hand. At the same time, push forward and down with your top hand. When the blade reaches your side, lift the paddle out of the water. Now you can repeat that stroke. Try to maintain a steady, even pace.

The back stroke is another common stroke. You probably guessed that it moves the boat backward. Using the same grip you used for the

Paddlers rely on teamwork to keep everyone safe!

forward stroke, extend the paddle straight back. Again, the farther back you place the blade, the more power you will have. Place the blade in the water and push forward. This tough move requires a lot of practice.

In a paddle raft, you will receive commands from the guide to drive the boat. The five basic commands are forward paddle, back paddle, right turn, left turn, and stop.

Paddling forward and backward in a raft are similar to the strokes used in canoeing.

Paddling is great exercise for your arms and upper body!

To turn, paddlers must know which side of the raft they are on and listen carefully. If the guide yells out for a left turn, paddlers on the left side of the boat back paddle. Those on the right side forward paddle. A stop command simply means everyone must stop paddling and take their paddles out of the water.

If you are kayaking, you will use a two-bladed paddle. To find the correct grip for you, place the middle of the paddle's shaft on the top of your head. Move your hands around until each elbow makes a 90-degree angle. One hand will be your control hand. It will keep a constant grip on the paddle. Between strokes, let the shaft rotate in your other hand.

To do the forward stroke in a kayak, rotate your torso as you paddle. Reach as far forward as you can to place one blade in the water. Then, pull back. Keep your bottom arm straight while the blade moves through the water. As that stroke ends, the other blade will be moving toward the water. Remove the first blade from the water. Then, begin the next stroke on the other side.

When kayaking, there are times you will need to reverse your course. Keep the same grip you used during the forward stroke. Turn your upper body as far to one side as you can. Place the blade in the water behind you. Push the blade forward until it reaches your toes. As the blade comes out of the water, rotate to place the other blade in the water on the other side.

Sometimes, you may have to stop quickly to avoid an obstacle such as a log or a rock. To stop, thrust one blade into the water next to your body. Pull the paddle out when you feel the water's pressure against the blade and the boat begins turning. Then, drop the other blade in the water on the opposite side. Again, remove the blade when you feel the water's pressure. Repeat these steps until the kayak stops.

Roll with It!

While paddling a raft through white water, you may fall out and need to be rescued! But if your kayak or canoe **capsizes**, you'll need to know how to roll instead. Paddlers should master how to flip their boats back over in case they ever find themselves upside down.

Rolling a canoe or a kayak is an essential skill. Once you get the hang of it, you'll be able to right yourself from inside your boat. This means you'll keep your lower body and the inside of your craft dry!

Many paddlers learn to roll in a kayak. The screw roll is the most common roll. Begin by holding the paddle along the boat's side with both hands. Next, overturn the kayak on the paddle side.

Once you are upside down under the water, remain calm. Make sure you still have both hands on the paddle. From bow to stern, sweep the paddle along the water's surface. While keeping your head down, use your leg muscles to help right the boat.

Capsizing can be scary. Your first instinct will be to get your head out of the water. But, your head should be the last body part to come out. That is why it is important to practice rolling. It will help you remain calm during a real-life situation.

Practice will help you build confidence in your rolling. While still on land, see how long you can hold your breath. Then, practice rolling in calm water.

Star Runners

Famous football and basketball players are often seen on television. Did you know there are famous runners, too? Michal Martikan of Slovakia has dominated the sport of men's canoe slalom singles. When he was just 16, Martikan won a World Cup in slalom racing. He has won the world championships five times. And he is a four-time Olympic medalist.

Dana Chladek broke new ground in women's single kayak white-water slalom racing. She is the first woman to win an Olympic medal in this event. Chladek won a bronze medal at the 1992 Summer Olympics. She won a silver medal at the 1996 games.

Dana Chladek

Few kayakers would dare to attempt the stunts Tao Berman does!

Sports Illustrated magazine called Tao Berman "the best known kayaker on the planet." Berman is famous for his daredevil, record-breaking descents. He set the world waterfall record at 98.4 feet (30 m).

Berman has also completed more than 50 first descents. He goes where no kayaker has gone before. Berman is the world's most extreme kayaker and shows no signs of letting up!

Where to Paddle

Do you want to learn to be a runner? The United States offers an abundance of world-class white-water runs. Some favorites are the Colorado River in Arizona and the Snake River in Idaho. On the East Coast, many paddlers enjoy the Cheat River in West Virginia and the Nantahala River in North Carolina. Internationally, Costa Rica and Chile have excellent white water. South Africa's Zambezi River is also popular.

Beginning runners should start with Class I rapids. It is very important not to overestimate your skill level when you are first learning. Taking a white-water tour is a good way to see if this activity is right for you. Tours can last a few hours to several days. They are a good way to get your feet wet!

White-water running is a great way to enjoy nature. And, you can exercise your body at the same time! The more you practice paddling, the better you will get. You will increase your speed and strength. Before you know it, you will be fearlessly running the rapids!

Running the rapids combines fun, friends, exercise, and the great outdoors all in one!

RESPECT THE RIVER!

Rafting, canoeing, and kayaking down clean, pristine rivers is wonderful! These natural wonders need your help to stay that way.

Plan ahead! Leave with everything you brought in and nothing more. That includes trash and gear. Don't take anything from your natural surroundings. Respect any wildlife you come across. Rivers are a resource that need protecting. Leave the outdoors as you found them, and they will stay beautiful and healthy for when you and others return.

Glossary

capsize - to turn over.

disqualify - to bar from competition or from winning a prize or a contest.

endurance - the ability to sustain a long, stressful effort or activity.

flexible - able to bend or move easily.

hazard - a source of danger.

inflatable - able to be expanded by filling with air or gas.

maneuver (muh-NOO-vuhr) - to make changes in direction and position for a specific purpose.

propel - to drive forward or onward by some force.

Web Sites

To learn more about white-water rafting, canoeing, and kayaking, visit ABDO Publishing Company online. Web sites about white-water rafting, canoeing, and kayaking are featured on our Book Links page. These like are routinely monitored and updated to provide the most current information available.
www.abdopublishing.com

Index